This Is My Planet

A Guide to
Global Warming

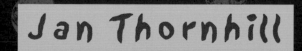

Jan Thornhill

First published in 2011
by Franklin Watts

Franklin Watts
338 Euston Road
London NW1 3BH

Franklin Watts Australia
Level 17/207 Kent Street
Sydney, NSW 2000

First published by Maple Tree Press Inc, 51 Front Street East,
Suite 200, Toronto, Ontario M5E 1B3
www.mapletreepress.com

Text © 2006 and 2011 Jan Thornhill

ISBN 978 0 7496 9483 8

Dewey number: 363.7'3874

Printed in China

Franklin Watts is a division of Hachette Children's Books,
an Hachette UK company.

www.hachette.co.uk

This book is printed on paper that has been
sustainably sourced.

Contents

This Is My Planet......................4

The Far North & South.........22

The Ocean.................................32

The Land...................................42

People..52

Further information...............63

Index..64

This Is My Planet

I love life
and
I love my
planet...

but

what about
global warming?

Is it really happening?

Why is it a problem?

Can we stop it?

How will it affect me?

In this book, we're going to try to answer
questions like these, and LOTS MORE...

But, if we're going to talk about global warming,

we also have to answer some questions about:

how our **Planet** works

Does Earth control its own temperature?

Are climate and weather the same thing?

How can we tell that Earth is warming up?

Our HOME
is Changing
and it's changing
FAST

Everywhere on Earth, **people are seeing change**. Arctic sea ice is melting earlier and forming later. Glaciers are disappearing. Heat waves are becoming more extreme — and so are storms and floods. And it's not only humans that are noticing these changes. Flowers are emerging sooner and insects are breeding faster. In some places, birds are laying their eggs before they're expected to and bears have stopped hibernating.

Earlier Starts

More Melting

So, what's going on? Well, our planet is getting warmer. In fact, its surface temperature has warmed about .7°C in the last century. This might seem like too small a change to worry about, but sometimes **little things can turn into big things.** Even a small increase in the temperature of our planet can change its climate. And when the climate changes, eventually all living things on Earth will be affected.

Wilder Weather

Part I
A Natural Greenhouse

Of all the planets in our solar system, Earth — as far as we know — is the only one that sustains **life**. So, what makes our little blue planet so special?

Sun
5,000˚C

Venus
482˚C

Earth
16˚C

Average Temperatures

Mars
-50˚C

The Sun's Energy

solar radiation   thermal radiation

Year in and year out the planets of our solar system warm up, they

Our Atmosphere

Our planet is surrounded by a layer of gases, including water vapour, that we call the atmosphere. The atmosphere **protects life** on Earth by absorbing ultraviolet solar radiation. It also keeps temperatures from rising too high during daylight hours and from getting too cold at night. More than half of all the gases and water in the atmosphere can be found below the peak of Mount Everest. The higher up you go, the thinner the atmosphere becomes. Weather systems, such as hurricanes, develop in the lower atmosphere, the part closest to the Earth.

Hurricane Emily

A hurricane, as seen from the space shuttle.

The Greenhouse Effect

The **greenhouse effect** is what we call the process that causes the surface of the Earth to be warmer than it would be if we had no atmosphere. This effect is produced when greenhouse gases, such as water vapour and carbon dioxide (CO_2), first allow solar radiation to pass through the atmosphere. But when heat radiates from the surface of the Earth, those same gases prevent most of it from escaping into outer space. Because we get heat from two sources, first, directly from the Sun, and second, from the atmosphere, the surface of the Earth is warmer than it would be without the greenhouse effect. Without this effect, most life on Earth could not exist.

The Sun's energy beams to Earth

Heat radiates from Earth

Gases keep heat from escaping

HOW EARTH WORKS Part II

Natural Cycles

Our planet is constantly changing. But even though it is always changing, there are **natural cycles** that work to keep Earth and its atmosphere in perfect balance.

The Carbon Cycle

Carbon is everywhere. It is in air, in water, in soil and rocks, and in all living things. But carbon doesn't stay still. It moves around. Plants take in carbon from the air in the form of carbon dioxide during the process of photosynthesis. When a rabbit eats a plant, it can then use the plant's carbon in its own body. When a fox eats a rabbit, it takes in carbon from the rabbit. Animals release carbon into the air when they breathe, and into the soil when they expel waste. They also release carbon when they die and decompose, and so do plants. Some plants don't decompose. Instead, over millions of years, they turn into fossil fuels such as oil and coal. By burning these fossil fuels, we release huge quantities of carbon — as carbon dioxide — into Earth's atmosphere.

Carbon in
Carbon out

Carbon Sinks

Places that hold vast stores of carbon and increase in size, such as forests and the ocean, are called "carbon sinks". "Sinks" are the opposite of "sources".

The Water Cycle

Precipitation — snow and rain

Water storage in atmosphere

Condensation — cooling vapour becomes liquid, forming clouds

Water storage in ice and snow

flow

Transpiration — plants release water through leaf pores

Evaporation — liquid changes to vapour

Water storage in icebergs and surface ice

Water storage in oceans and lakes

We are surrounded by water. Although most of it is in our oceans, it's also in our bodies and in the air we breathe. It fills lakes and rivers and vast underground reservoirs. It lies frozen in glaciers and in the ice caps of the poles. But the amount of water on Earth is limited. The same water just keeps **moving around and around**. This movement is called the water cycle.

All of the water on Earth has been moving around in a cycle for 3.5 billion years. This means that the water vapour in the air you are breathing right now could once have been in the lungs of a dinosaur. Or it could have been part of the rain that once put out a Neanderthal's cooking fire. It could even have been part of the iceberg that sank the *Titanic*!

Do I Need a Jumper?

Weather is what is happening with the atmosphere outside. But weather isn't the same thing as climate. Climate is the big picture. It's the **pattern** of weather that we expect to see in a particular place.

Weather

Most of us think of weather in terms of how warm or cold it is, how cloudy or windy, or whether it's raining or snowing. But no matter what the weather is like outside, it's always driven by the Sun's energy. Warm air is constantly being moved by the atmosphere to places where it's cold, while cold air is constantly being moved to places that are warm. This **circulation of warm and cold air**, combined with the movement of the oceans and the amount of moisture there is in the air, creates everything from perfect sunny days to hail storms to tornadoes and hurricanes.

Climate

Weather changes frequently, but from year to year the climate of a particular place should stay about the same. For instance, people who live in northern parts of the world expect it to be cold in the winter. That doesn't mean that every single day of the winter will be freezing. It means that when all of the temperatures over a winter are looked at together, the **average** temperature will be cold. People have these same expectations of different climates all over the world.

Polar

- low temperature
- strong winds
- year-round snow

Temperate

- changeable weather
- distinct seasons
- cold winters

Mountains

- create own climate
- cold at peaks
- warmer below

Prairie

- warm summers
- cold winters
- possible droughts

Tropical

- high temperatures
- regular heavy rains
- often cloudy or humid

Monsoon

- half of year dry
- seasonal rains
- frequent flooding

Coastal

- year-round precipitation
- moderate temperatures
- moist air

Hot Deserts

- hot days, cold nights
- clear skies
- little rain

The Big Picture

Earth's climate has changed many times over millions of years. **Ice Ages** occur regularly — lately about once every 100,000 years. These glacial cold periods are followed by much warmer periods, such as the Cretaceous era, when dinosaurs roamed the Earth. Right now, we're still recovering from the last Ice Age about 12,000 years ago. So we can expect that world temperatures will continue to rise over time. What is worrying is that Earth's surface temperatures seem to be rising faster now than they were a hundred years ago.

It's All About
Balance

Our planet is always changing. As it changes, its systems are always working together to keep a kind of **balance**. All forms of life, including humans, depend on this balance being kept.

Carbon
Atmosphere
Climate
Energy
Living things
Water Cycle

The Web of Life

Living things are connected to one another in **ecosystems** by food chains and food webs. Plants get energy directly from the Sun through the process of photosynthesis. Herbivores get energy by eating plants. Carnivores get theirs by eating animals. To see how energy flows through an ecosystem, start at the Sun and then follow the arrows through this northern, or boreal, forest food web. What would happen if all the trees died, or all the insects?

When Things Go Wrong

uh oh!

Broken Links

In the early 1950s, the pesticide DDT was sprayed on the island of Borneo to kill mosquitoes carrying malaria, a dangerous disease. The mosquitoes died, but so did other insects. Little lizards called geckoes ate the poisoned insects, and then *they* died. House cats ate the geckoes, and then *they* died, too. With no cats to control them, the island's rat population exploded. These rats brought even more dangerous diseases to the islanders. The DDT spraying had to stop, and healthy cats had to be brought in. Some villages were so remote that cats had to be dropped in by parachute!

BANG!

The Year Without Summer

In April 1815, Mount Tambora in Indonesia blew her top. It was the most **colossal volcanic eruption** in recorded history. Thousands were killed. Over the following year, massive amounts of ash and gases spread around the globe, causing temperatures worldwide to fall by 3°C. Snow storms hit eastern North America in June and widespread frost killed crops in August. Huge storms caused flooding in Europe and China. Tree growth slowed. All around the world, humans and other animals suffered from shortages of food. So what if the opposite happened? What would be the effects if the world warmed up a lot?

What will happen in a warmer world?

The Temperature's Rising

Amazingly, the **eleven hottest years** in the past century have all occurred since 1995. Unquestionably, our world is getting warmer.

Rising Temperatures

Over the past hundred years, global **surface temperatures** have risen by 0.6°C — and they're still rising. Climate scientists are predicting that over the next century world temperatures will go up another 1.5°C, or possibly even higher. Warmer temperatures will speed up the water cycle, which will increase the possibility of heavy precipitation, droughts and wild-fires. It's also very likely that extreme heat waves will become more common.

Greenhouse Gases

Greenhouse gases in the atmosphere absorb radiant energy from the Earth's surface, and then emit some of it back down again. Greenhouse gases include water vapour, carbon dioxide, methane, ozone and nitrous oxide. The amounts of these gases in the atmosphere have stayed stable for thousands of years. But over the past century, concentrations of some of these greenhouse gases have **increased dramatically**. This increase seems to be magnifying the greenhouse effect.

Shrinking Sea Ice

Since the last **Ice Age**, a large portion of the Arctic has been covered in ice. During the winter this ice increases, and each summer, the same amount melts. At least, that's what used to happen. Now scientists are finding that not only does more of this sea ice thaw each year, but the ice that forms in the winter is not nearly as thick or as extensive as it once was.

Abnormal Precipitation

Warmer air increases evaporation. In the hottest parts of the world, closer to the equator, this can affect rainfall and increase the likelihood of **drought**. Though drought is not as much of a problem towards the poles, in these areas there may be an increase in dramatic weather events, such as uncommonly **heavy rain**. Intense precipitation can cause soil erosion, flooding, landslides and damage to property. More severe hurricane and typhoon seasons can also be expected with the warming of the world's oceans.

Sea Levels Rising

The rate that sea levels are now rising is at least **three times faster** than it was a century ago. This is partly because the oceans are warming, and warming water expands. The melting of glaciers and polar ice sheets is also contributing to the increase. Rising sea levels worsen the risk of erosion, flooding and salt water contamination of drinking water. Scientists think the sea levels will continue to rise for at least another hundred years.

Melting Glaciers

Glaciers are moving rivers of ice. They exist on every continent, even Australia. Most have been around since the end of the last Ice Age, but now they're disappearing. Over the past century, a startling number of mountain glaciers have been losing more ice each summer than they gain in the winter. As a result, they are substantially **decreasing in size**. If they continue to retreat at the same rate, up to a quarter of all glacier ice in the world will have melted away by 2050.

Greenhouse Gases

Greenhouse gases help to keep our world from being either too hot or too cold. But the amounts of some greenhouse gases in the atmosphere are increasing. Most scientists think these gases are enhancing the **greenhouse effect** and are making our planet warmer.

 Natural Source

Human Source

H₂O – Water Vapour

Water vapour in the atmosphere causes most of the natural greenhouse effect. Human activity does not directly affect the amount of moisture in the atmosphere, but an increase in temperatures will cause more water to evaporate, which, in turn, will increase the greenhouse effect. Water vapour enters the atmosphere through **evaporation** and **sublimation**.

Sublimation is a process that causes a solid, such as ice, to turn into a gas without first turning to a liquid. This is the same process that makes ice cubes in a freezer shrink over time.

CO₂ – Carbon Dioxide

Carbon dioxide is a major greenhouse gas. Astonishingly, its levels in the atmosphere have risen by more than a third since the Industrial Revolution began in the late 1700s. These levels could remain high for hundreds of years. CO_2 enters the atmosphere as part of the natural **carbon cycle**, but we are now adding huge amounts more, mostly through deforestation and the burning of fossil fuels.

Volcanoes have always spewed CO_2 into the atmosphere, and so have animals when they breathe. Humans burning fossil fuels is a new source.

CH$_4$ – Methane

Methane is **a form of carbon**. It is released naturally by animals including termites and cattle, as well as the oceans, peat bogs and mud volcanoes. Though there is less methane than CO_2 in the atmosphere, it packs a punch as a greenhouse gas with 20 times the effect of CO_2. Humans are responsible for about half of today's emissions, mostly from landfills, keeping livestock and natural gas production.

bund 25% of waste in the UK is buried landfill sites. As it breaks down, this ste releases methane.

As part of their digestion process, livestock such as cattle and sheep belch out a fifth of all human-related methane.

Bacteria in oceans and in moist forest soils naturally produce nitrous oxide.

N$_2$O – Nitrous Oxide

Nitrous oxide, also known as "laughing gas", is about 300 times as effective as carbon dioxide at trapping heat in the atmosphere, so it's a very powerful greenhouse gas. Natural emissions of nitrous oxide come from the oceans and from bacteria breaking down nitrogen in soils. Humans are responsible for the emissions produced by agriculture, as well as by industry.

The main sources of human-produced nitrous oxide are fertiliser and animal manure.

19

Measuring Change

If we're going to understand what's going on with the world's climate we need to find as much **information** as we can about what happened in the past.

Ancient Clues

Paleoclimatologists are climate history detectives. They look for clues about the past in a variety of natural recorders, such as plant pollens and the growth rings of trees and corals. Another place they look is in the ancient ice of Greenland and Antarctica. Scientists, like the ones shown above, drill deep into the ice and extract cores. These ice cores have distinct yearly layers that scientists can count. Ice also traps tiny bubbles of air as it forms. These bubbles can tell scientists what levels of greenhouse gases were in the atmosphere when the ice was created. Some ice-core samples are 700,000 years old!

The varying widths of the annual growth rings of trees offer scientists clues about climate history.

Pollen grains found at the bottom of lakes and oceans offer clues to what kinds of plants were growing when the pollen was deposited.

Corals grow in distinct yearly layers that vary depending on temperature.

Coincidence?

The graph below shows how the ups and downs of the **world's temperatures** (in red) and **carbon dioxide levels** (in green) closely match one another. In only 100 years, CO_2 levels have risen much higher than at any other time in the past 400,000 years. Because we know that temperatures go up with rising CO_2 levels, we can expect the world to continue to warm for quite some time.

eek!

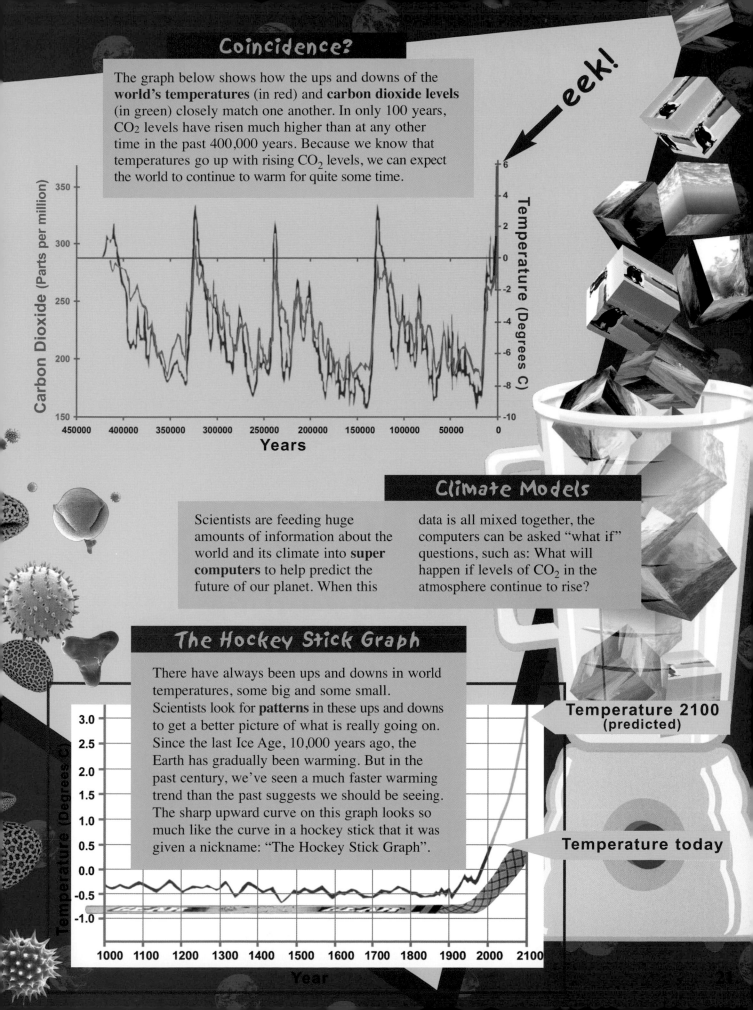

Carbon Dioxide (Parts per million)

350

300

250

200

150

450000 400000 350000 300000 250000 200000 150000 100000 50000 0

Years

Temperature (Degrees C)

6
4
2
0
-2
-4
-6
-8
-10

Climate Models

Scientists are feeding huge amounts of information about the world and its climate into **super computers** to help predict the future of our planet. When this data is all mixed together, the computers can be asked "what if" questions, such as: What will happen if levels of CO_2 in the atmosphere continue to rise?

The Hockey Stick Graph

There have always been ups and downs in world temperatures, some big and some small. Scientists look for **patterns** in these ups and downs to get a better picture of what is really going on. Since the last Ice Age, 10,000 years ago, the Earth has gradually been warming. But in the past century, we've seen a much faster warming trend than the past suggests we should be seeing. The sharp upward curve on this graph looks so much like the curve in a hockey stick that it was given a nickname: "The Hockey Stick Graph".

Temperature 2100 (predicted)

Temperature today

Temperature (Degrees C)

3.0
2.5
2.0
1.5
1.0
0.5
0.0
-0.5
-1.0

1000 1100 1200 1300 1400 1500 1600 1700 1800 1900 2000 2100

Year

The Far North & South

Strange but true: the most warming is being seen in Earth's coldest places.

BIG things

are happening to...

The Far North & South includes the Arctic, Antarctica, Alaska, Canada's Territories and parts of Scandinavia and Russia.

...traditions

...ancient ice

...seasons

...wildlife

...habitats

Far North & South
What We See Now

Arctic temperatures are rising **twice as fast** as elsewhere on the planet. So what's going on?

Something Called Albedo

Albedo is a measure of the amount of the Sun's energy that is reflected back into space. Darker parts of the Earth, such as oceans and forests, have low **albedo**, so they reflect only a small portion of the Sun's energy. Lighter-coloured ice, snow and clouds have high albedo, so they reflect more. When snow and ice melt, revealing land and ocean, the albedo changes from high to low, which causes more of the Sun's energy to be absorbed. This can cause a **positive feed-back response**, which means that the decrease in albedo in areas where polar ice is melting will lead to further warming, which will then lower albedo even more, which will increase warming — and so on and so on and so on.

High Albedo
- ice & snow
- clouds
- sand

Low Albedo
- open water
- plant growth
- dark rock

Disappearing Ice

These two pictures, based on satellite images of the Arctic ice cap, show the average minimum amount of ice in the summers of 1979–81 and 2003–05. Though some of this ice loss is probably caused by natural changes in the Arctic climate, global warming seems to be the main culprit. As the sea ice disappears, not only does the albedo change from high to low, warmer water begins to flow in. When this happens, the loss of ice keeps increasing.

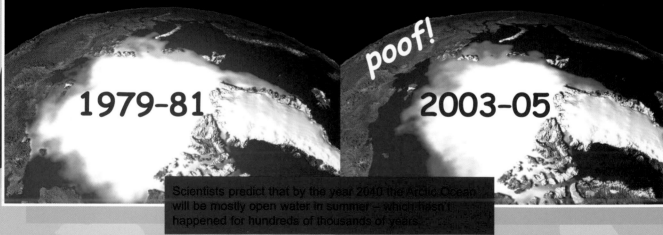

1979-81

poof!

2003-05

Scientists predict that by the year 2040 the Arctic Ocean will be mostly open water in summer – which hasn't happened for hundreds of thousands of years.

Disintegrating Ice

In 2002, scientists around the world were alarmed when Larsen B, a massive 10,000-year-old ice shelf in Antarctica, suddenly disintegrated. Ice shelves normally lose bits of their edges when icebergs break off, or "calve", but they don't just suddenly collapse. Most scientists think the collapse was caused by warmer temperatures. Since ice shelves float on the surface of the ocean, there is no change in sea level when they break off. But ice shelves act as a **braking system** for ice sheets on land, so their loss speeds the flow of glaciers (see page 17) into the ocean, which *does* raise sea levels. An up side to the collapse is that an international expedition of scientists has finally been able to get a good look at what lies beneath ice shelves. Not only will they be able to monitor how a specific ecosystem adapts to global warming, they've already discovered at least **30 new species**!

Even the tiniest floating pieces in this satellite picture of the break-up of Larsen B shelf are icebergs!

These are only three of the new species found in the Antarctic ocean.

Not So Permanent Permafrost

permanently frozen layer

Thawing permafrost is making ponds appear that never existed before, while others drain away.

25

Far North & South

Effects on Living Things

The Far North and South both have very

When one link in a food chain is altered, the effects are quickly seen elsewhere.

Teeny Weeny Sea Creatures

Krill are shrimp-like creatures that eat **plankton**, the tiny plants and animals at the bottom of the ocean **food chain**. In the Antarctic, krill feed on plankton that live under sea ice. But the ice is disappearing — and so are the krill. Scientists are now finding only one fifth the number of krill than they did 30 years ago. This spells trouble for the many fish, birds and whales that eat them.

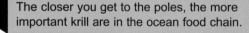
The closer you get to the poles, the more important krill are in the ocean food chain.

Penguins

Antarctic **Adelie penguins** are used to walking long distances from the water to their breeding grounds. But in recent years, warming of the oceans has caused changes in sea-ice movement, and some colonies of Adelies are now having to travel so far by foot that they arrive too late at their nesting grounds to successfully rear young. Meanwhile, in other parts of the Antarctic, Adelies are thriving because fish stocks have grown as the water has warmed.

Polar Bears

Polar bears spend most of their lives on sea ice, hunting for seals and other sea mammals. When this ice melts in the summer, polar bears move to land where they survive on fat stored in their bodies. Unfortunately, Arctic sea ice is melting earlier and freezing later. Abnormally large expanses of water are ending up ice-free, which, in turn, is reducing the polar bears' seal-hunting season. This could be a problem because low-weight females don't seem able to produce cubs.

Actual Size

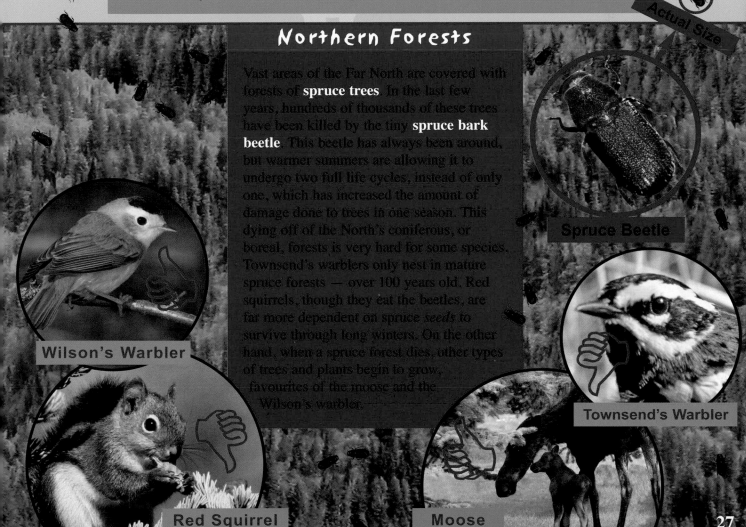

Northern Forests

Vast areas of the Far North are covered with forests of **spruce trees**. In the last few years, hundreds of thousands of these trees have been killed by the tiny **spruce bark beetle**. This beetle has always been around, but warmer summers are allowing it to undergo two full life cycles, instead of only one, which has increased the amount of damage done to trees in one season. This dying off of the North's coniferous, or boreal, forests is very hard for some species. Townsend's warblers only nest in mature spruce forests — over 100 years old. Red squirrels, though they eat the beetles, are far more dependent on spruce *seeds* to survive through long winters. On the other hand, when a spruce forest dies, other types of trees and plants begin to grow, favourites of the moose and the Wilson's warbler.

Spruce Beetle

Wilson's Warbler

Townsend's Warbler

Red Squirrel

Moose

27

Far North & South
Further Warming

Because the Arctic and Antarctic regions are **warming the fastest**, what happens in the future could be much more extreme than elsewhere.

If Greenland Melts

Greenland's ice cap is the second largest in the world, and it may be melting faster than anyone thought. What scientists have found is that **ice sheets crack** as the surface warms. Melt water quickly trickles down through the cracks until it reaches the bottom, where ice meets rock. This water "greases" the way for the ice to slide faster into the sea. If all of Greenland's ice melted, it would raise the sea level 6.5 metres. Adding all that lighter fresh water to the ocean could also change the flow of major currents. A change in currents could drastically alter the climate of Europe.

Polar Mammals

Many Arctic mammals are dependent on ice. They have their young on ice, they travel to find food on ice and they rest on ice. Walrus mothers leave their pups on ice floes while they forage for food. With less and less ice, pups that are not yet strong swimmers end up in the water and sometimes get separated from their mothers before they are able to find their own food. The Arctic ice is disappearing so rapidly that species such as the **walrus, seal** and **polar bear** may not be able to adapt and may face extinction.

When plants flower earlier, they also bear fruit earlier.

On the Move

Already, **birds** and **insects** that have never been seen so far north are surprising people in the Arctic — species that will compete with native animals for food. Plants are beginning to flower earlier, and melting permafrost is reducing the amount of pale lichen that reflects the Sun's energy. The tree-line is also creeping northward onto the tundra. Though trees take in a lot of carbon, which is good, they are dark, and the more of them there are in an area, the less albedo (see page 24) the area has. We don't yet know how all of these changes will affect Arctic ecosystems.

In the Arctic the North American robin is an exotic newcomer.

Pale lichens keep the ground cool by reflecting sunlight.

For Peat's Sake

Peat bogs are accumulations of dead plant matter that hasn't fully decayed. Up to a third of the world's soil carbon might be stored in peat bogs, so they are a huge **carbon sink** (see page 10). The Far North has vast areas of peat bogs that have been frozen since the last Ice Age. But now, with the thawing of permafrost, scientists are concerned that massive quantities of carbon, in the form of methane, may suddenly be released into the atmosphere, worsening global warming.

Peat stores a lot of carbon. It can be harvested and used as a fuel.

Sea Birds

Many **millions of birds** migrate to the Arctic each spring to breed. But a warmer Arctic means that their breeding grounds will change. The timing of the birds' arrival may no longer coincide with the insect food sources they expect to find. Rising sea levels and ponds draining away will alter wetland habitats. For sea birds, changes in water temperature and currents have already interfered with their food sources, causing some to starve and others to abandon their young.

Almost a million auklets abandoned their Arctic nests in 2005 when their normal ocean food didn't arrive on time.

Far North & South

The Human Side...

Because the effects of global warming are strongest in the Far North, **the people** who live there notice changes every day.

Native Peoples

Native peoples of the Far North have unique **age-old knowledge** of their land and climate, and of the behaviour of the animals they have always hunted. But global warming is changing their lives. Nothing is predictable anymore. Weather signs have become more difficult to read. Melting permafrost and thinning ice are making it more difficult, and more dangerous, for hunters to move around, and seals are disappearing from traditional hunting areas, following the ice north.

Caribou numbers are expected to drop drastically as snow surfaces change with warming, making it more difficult for them to feed in the winter. Underweight females are much less likely to successfully raise young.

People have begun catching salmon, never before seen so far north.

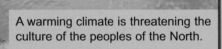

A warming climate is threatening the culture of the peoples of the North.

Washed Away

The patterns of wind, temperature, ice and currents have been changing in the North. Winds are stronger and have been driving damaging ice against the shore. A longer ice-free season leaves the coastline unprotected from waves for longer periods each year. Permafrost is also thawing along the coast. These things combined are causing a sharp **increase in erosion**. In some places, whole communities, some 400 years old, are facing evacuation before the sea washes them away.

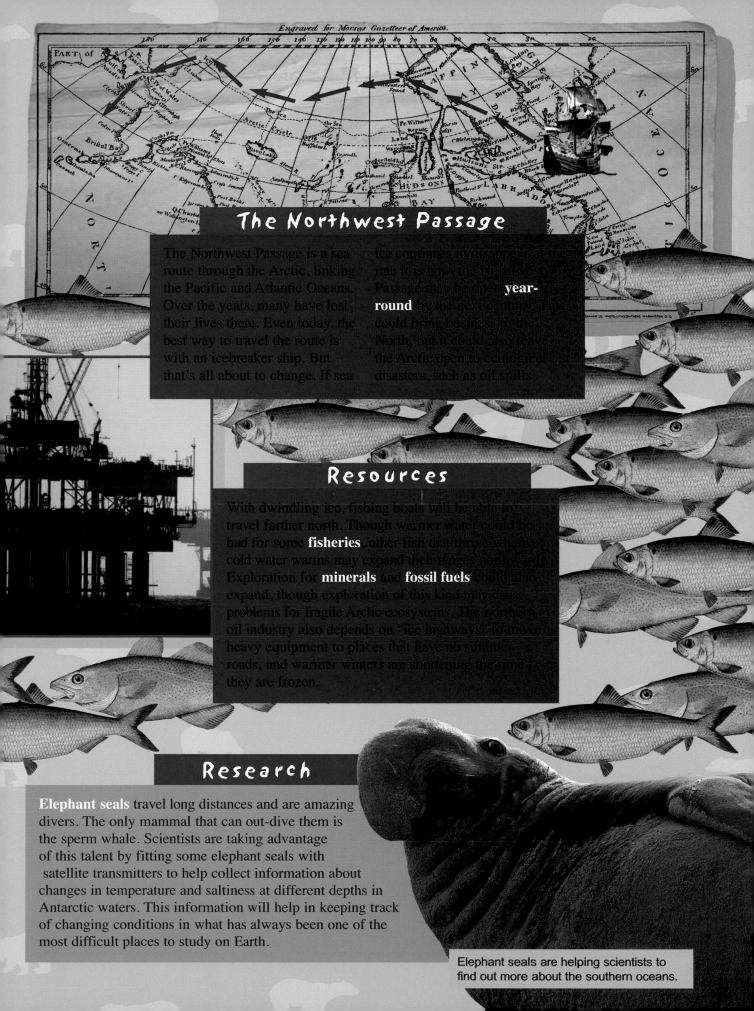

The Northwest Passage

The Northwest Passage is a sea route through the Arctic, linking the Pacific and Atlantic Oceans. Over the years, many have lost their lives there. Even today, the best way to travel the route is with an icebreaker ship. But that's all about to change. If sea ice continues to disappear at the rate it is now, the Northwest Passage may be open **year-round** by the next century. This could bring business to the North, but it could also leave the Arctic open to ecological disasters, such as oil spills.

Resources

With dwindling ice, fishing boats will be able to travel farther north. Though warmer water could be bad for some **fisheries**, other fish that thrive when cold water warms may expand their ranges northward. Exploration for **minerals** and **fossil fuels** could also expand, though exploration of this kind may cause problems for fragile Arctic ecosystems. The northern oil industry also depends on "ice highways" to move heavy equipment to places that have no summer roads, and warmer winters are shortening the time they are frozen.

Research

Elephant seals travel long distances and are amazing divers. The only mammal that can out-dive them is the sperm whale. Scientists are taking advantage of this talent by fitting some elephant seals with satellite transmitters to help collect information about changes in temperature and saltiness at different depths in Antarctic waters. This information will help in keeping track of changing conditions in what has always been one of the most difficult places to study on Earth.

Elephant seals are helping scientists to find out more about the southern oceans.

The Ocean

Most of our planet's surface is covered by a single ocean — the World Ocean, and it's...

...HUGE

...and beautiful

...and mysterious...

changes in living communities

...but we're seeing changes in it

changes in ocean chemistry

higher sea levels

more violent storms

The Ocean
What We See Now

Even though the World Ocean covers more than three-quarters of Earth's surface, we are only just beginning to understand it.

Currents

Our planet has a number of ways of controlling its temperature. One of these is through interconnected ocean currents. These currents act as a **conveyor belt**, moving warm water to cold places, and cold water to warm places. As water is moved towards the poles, it becomes cooler, saltier and denser. This makes it heavier, so it sinks down to the ocean bottom. Warmer water moves in to take its place, keeping the "conveyor belt" going. Because fresh water is lighter than salt water, the constant addition of rain and melting ice mixing with sea water also helps to drive the conveyer.

How Rubber Duckies Are Helping Scientists

In 1992, 29,000 rubber bath toys fell off a ship in the middle of the Pacific during a storm. Scientists have been learning more about ocean currents by following the progress of these floating ducks, turtles, frogs and beavers.

Ocean Chemistry

Water is good at dissolving substances, salt being the most obvious one. Seawater also dissolves gases, particularly carbon dioxide. In fact, **most of the world's carbon** is held in the ocean in this form. Some is used by trillions of tiny plants, called phytoplankton, during photosynthesis. When plankton die, they drift to the bottom, taking carbon with them. The ocean is therefore another important carbon sink.

People consume 45 million tonnes of salt a year, much of it coming from the sea.

Micro-communities

Trillions of microscopic plankton are the first links in the ocean food chain. **Phytoplankton** — tiny plants — take CO_2 from the water during photosynthesis. **Zooplankton** are mini-animals. In a simple ocean food chain, phytoplankton are eaten by zooplankton, which are then eaten by krill, which are then eaten by fish, which are then eaten by sea birds. Even small changes in plankton numbers or movements can echo up through the food chain and tip the balance of an ecosystem. And because the ocean is warming, some of these changes are already being seen.

Copepods are a type of zooplankton.

There may be more copepods in the ocean than all the other multi-celled animals in the world combined!

Warmer Water and Carbon

Because **sea water dissolves carbon dioxide**, the ocean actually removes huge amounts of human-produced CO_2 from the air. But cold water is better at dissolving gases than warm water and the ocean is warming, so its intake of CO_2 may slow. Added to this, if there are big changes in the populations of CO_2-gobbling phytoplankton — changes already being seen in some places — the constant movement of carbon down to the bottom of the ocean may also slow. Another worrying possibility is that changes in ocean circulation could cause vast quantities of carbon stored at the bottom to be brought to the top and released into the atmosphere.

Limestone, one of the world's most important carbon sinks, is made from the shells of sea creatures that settle at the bottom of the ocean.

Sea Level Rise

In the past 100 years the world sea level has risen by 10–25 cm, mostly because **warm water expands**. Even if there is not substantial melting of glaciers and the ice sheets of Greenland, scientists are predicting at least a doubling of those numbers in the next hundred years. Just a small rise in sea levels increases erosion and the chance of flooding. Areas most at risk are coastal lowlands, wetlands, beaches and small islands.

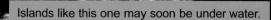
Islands like this one may soon be under water.

The Ocean
Effects on Living Things

The World Ocean is home to incredibly **complex ecosystems** that are easily upset.

Wee Beasties

Trillions of **phytoplankton**, the first link in the ocean food chain, take in CO_2 to use in the process of photosynthesis. There are so many of these little things drifting around near the surface of the ocean that they absorb about **100 million tonnes** of CO_2 each day! But these mini-plants become less productive as their environment warms. Their numbers fall, and this, in turn, affects living things all the way up the ocean food chain.

Phytoplankton called diatoms are probably the biggest oxygen producers in the world. Over 100,000 species have already been identified.

Coral Reefs

About a quarter of all ocean fish species can be found in coral reef ecosystems. The skeletons of corals, made out of calcium and CO_2, are the "backbone" of reefs. Corals are **colonies** of small animals, called polyps, that live together with **tiny algae**. The algae help the corals get food, and are responsible for the amazing colours of healthy corals. When corals get too warm, they expel the algae and lose their colours, or "bleach". If the water doesn't cool, the corals can die. A dead reef cannot support the diversity of life that thrives around living coral.

Sea Turtles

Sea turtles spend their whole lives at sea — except when females return to the same beaches where they hatched to lay their own eggs. Rising sea levels could cause many of these beaches to disappear. Just as bad, only a little warming of beach sand can affect the number of eggs that hatch.

Sea Mammals

The numbers of some whales are dropping because there are fewer krill for them to eat. **Orcas** may soon face a similar problem as salmon numbers fall. On the other hand, female grey **seals** are travelling further in search of drinking water. As a result, more males are mating with them, which is good for the gene-pool of their species, and may help them adapt to climate change.

Fish Stocks

More than half of all people depend on the ocean for animal protein. But these ocean animals are in trouble. Though the worst problem is human over-fishing – taking more fish than a particular population can tolerate – now **warming oceans** are adding to the problem. One of the things ocean food chains depend on is the movement of plankton-rich waters. But some of these expected movements are changing. This could cause food shortages and not just for fish, but for millions of people, too.

The Aliens Are Coming!

Warmer waters are encouraging some species to move from their usual territories into areas they've never visited before. Humans are also introducing species to new places. Often, there are **no natural enemies** to stop these invasive species from multiplying like crazy and they can take over an ecosystem like a weed, pushing out the original inhabitants.

The Ocean
Further Warming

Because it's so vast, the ocean is difficult to study. Though we're not sure exactly how it will behave as it gets warmer, some changes might be unavoidable.

Rising Sea Levels

One tenth of the world's population lives within 10 metres above sea level. The minimum rise in sea levels predicted for 2100 will affect millions of these people, mostly in the world's poorest places where there is little money for flood protection. If there is serious melting of the ice sheets of the Antarctic or Greenland, major cities around the world could be threatened. Coastal areas at risk need to move development inland, build flood barriers, and protect natural buffers, such as mangrove forests and salt marshes. The world community also needs to make plans to help the millions of climate-change refugees that rising sea levels could create.

In low-lying Bangladesh, more than 10 million people may have to find new homes if nothing is done to slow global warming.

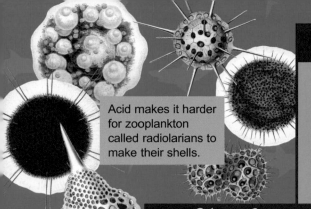

Acid makes it harder for zooplankton called radiolarians to make their shells.

To see what even a weak acid can do to a calcium shell, try this simple experiment:

Step 1. Submerge a raw egg in its shell in a bowl of household vinegar.

Step 2. Leave it for a week. And that's it!

Chemistry Changes

The ocean is now taking in more CO_2 than it has in hundreds of thousands of years. All that CO_2 is making the oceans **more acidic**. Because acid dissolves calcium, corals in a more acidic ocean would grow more slowly. Many zooplankton and other sea animals would either have trouble making their protective shells, or their shells would dissolve.

Hurricanes

Though it's impossible to blame any single event, such as Hurricane Katrina which hit the US in August 2005 with devastating results, on global warming, it is likely that hurricanes will become **more severe** as the ocean warms. This is because there is a strong connection between surface water temperatures and the power of hurricanes. A combination of warm water and the unstable lower atmosphere that warm water creates is the source of a hurricane's energy. So the warmer the water gets, the stronger, and more damaging, a hurricane can become.

Hurricane Katrina was so powerful she swept these boats onto a road.

Conveyor Belt Shutdown

Some scientists believe that if enough fresh water from melting glaciers and surface ice is added to the ocean, it could affect the **ocean's currents**. The Gulf Stream is a warm ocean current which flows across the Atlantic from the eastern US to Europe. If it shuts down, or changes course, temperatures in Europe could drop by 10ºC.

The Ocean

The Human Side...

Though scientists believe there will be changes to **Earth's oceans**, there are things we can do to help — both for ourselves and for the thousands of species that call the ocean home.

Spiny lobsters migrate in long lines.

Turbines will soon be turning ocean energy into electricity.

A Helping Hand

It's expected that as the oceans warm, **sea life will migrate** to cooler waters. To allow these animals to travel safely, fishing-free zones need to be established. Also, because healthy plants and animals are more able to adapt to changes to their habitats, it will be more important than ever to reduce pollution, and to stop destructive fishing practices, such as bottom trawling, where heavy nets are dragged along the sea floor.

Water Power

New technologies are going to tap an ocean source for renewable energy — **tidal movement** and **ocean currents**. Some of these technologies will use rows of underwater turbines set into the sea floor in places where there are high currents. These will work much the same as wind turbines, but because water is much denser than air, even slow-moving water will generate a lot of power.

Coral Reefs

Some scientists think that bleached corals might accept new, warm-water tolerant algae after they eject their old algae partners. Other scientists are growing coral colonies in "nurseries", and then using **glue** to transplant these corals to damaged reefs.

Sand Dunes

Mangroves

DAMAGE CONTROL

Salt Marshes

Beach Grasses

Long before the arrival of humans, the sea rose and fell, and there were hurricanes and tsunamis. Coastal environments have **evolved to survive** these kinds of assaults. Mangrove forests of the tropics are not only a crucial nursery for young reef fish that thrive amongst the tangle of underwater roots, they also protect the land from the ocean. Salt marshes work in the same way, taking the brunt of storm surges and protecting inland areas from flooding. Sand dunes also offer protection from storms, and dunes, in turn, are saved from erosion by hardy beach grasses. To take advantage of what these natural coastal environments can do for us, we need to slow down coastal development all around the world.

The Land

Most humans on Earth live on land. I live on land. And I expect you do, too.

forest loss

But we're seeing changes on land...

species at risk

deserts
growing

wildfires

increasing CO₂
emissions

What We See Now

Rising temperatures and longer periods of drought are causing even bigger problems.

Wildfire

All over the world — from Portugal to Indonesia, from Canada to Australia — wildfires have been increasing in frequency, strength and expanse. These fires cause massive loss of plant life and millions of pounds of damage. But worse, because plants trap and store carbon, when they burn, huge amounts of CO_2 billow into the atmosphere.

During the "Dust Bowl" of the 1930s in western North America, years of drought caused severe hardship for thousands of people.

Growing Deserts

Almost two billion people live in the dry lands on the fringes of deserts. In many of these places, drier conditions are allowing wind to blow away topsoil. As the soil loses its fertility, it becomes more and more difficult for healthy plants to grow and hold soil in place. With this type of erosion, it doesn't take long before once fertile land has turned into barren desert. Practising low-intensity farming in these areas, and planting coarse grasses, shrubs and trees can help stop deserts from growing.

Poof! ...a glacier disappears

1938   1981   1998   2005

Like other glaciers, this one in Montana, USA is almost gone.

Bit by bit, Glaciers Are Melting

Glaciers include the massive ice sheets of Greenland and Antarctica. Every year, glaciers gain ice from compressed snow, and lose ice when some of that snow then thaws. A billion people around the world depend in some way on mountain glacier melt water. But now, in many places, more glacier ice is melting in the summer than is being replaced in the winter. Everywhere in the world, the glaciers are shrinking and some have almost disappeared.

Healthy vegetation is bright red in this satellite image.

This isn't an abstract painting — it's a satellite picture showing with infrared light what deforestation in the Amazonian rainforest of Bolivia really looks like.

Deforestation

Every second, a chunk of forest the size of a football field is cut down or burned. Not only are forests of all kinds major carbon sinks, many forests create their own rain as part of their water cycle. In the Amazon rainforest in South America, trees use only a little of the rainwater they suck up through their roots. The rest is released into the air through pores in their leaves. In the Amazon and other rainforests, this water vapour gathers together in the atmosphere and creates rain. Without the trees, the rain disappears, leaving little chance for the forest to regenerate.

The star-like shapes are farm fields fanning out from small communities.

A third of all land species are found in the Amazon rainforest.

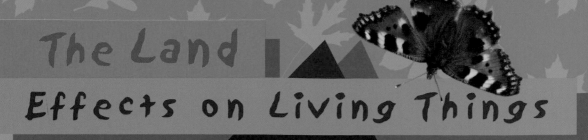

The Land
Effects on Living Things

Healthy ecosystems are made up of all kinds of animals and plants that interact in many different ways. Even a small change in climate can affect the way ecosystems work.

Warmer winters are allowing plants, such as holly, to creep northwards.

On the Move

Plant and insect species are already responding to warming. Alpine, or mountain plants, are moving upwards, and, in both North America and Europe, the breeding ranges of numerous insects are shifting northwards. Scientists are not sure yet, but insects and plants moving into new territories will likely cause stress for species that already call those places home.

In Europe, the breeding ranges of 22 of 35 butterfly species studied have shifted northwards.

Alpine plants are moving upwards — but they can't move higher than a mountain's peak!

Birds

Already, many species of bird are moving further north and are laying eggs earlier. These changes can be a problem when, for instance, the timing of insect hatches is out of sync with when the birds need to find them to eat. But warming appears to be working in favour of at least one species: swallows, like the ones below, are not only nesting earlier in Denmark, they're taking more time before laying their second brood, and having more success in rearing their young.

The British whitethroat faces a longer migration every winter as it has to travel further north to its breeding grounds.

Mammals

The winter of 2006 was so warm that mountain bears in Spain decided not to hibernate. As the planet heats up, other mammals are expected to respond as well. But, unlike birds and many insects, most mammals can't fly, so shifting ranges won't be so easy.

Scientists who have studied other major climate change events in the past predict that if warming speeds up, particularly in combination with human-caused loss of habitat, a large number of mammal species will be lost to us forever.

Not only are some red squirrels having babies earlier in the spring, but their female offspring are doing the same. This could be evidence of climate-driven evolution.

Climate change may be the last straw for the Bengal tiger.

47

The Land

Further Warming

Climate change will affect all living things on the planet, including humans.

Water Shortages

All humans need fresh water to survive. But scientists are predicting serious changes in rainfall patterns, along with loss of melt water from glaciers. Droughts will become more severe. Crops will fail. People will go hungry, mostly in places where millions already live in poverty. Because hungry people will move to find what they need, there could be hundreds of thousands of people leaving their homes in search of water and food. Before this happens, countries with plenty will have to plan how they will help these people — by supplying food, technology and other assistance, as well as by taking in refugees.

The 700,000 people who live in this small section of Nairobi, Kenya, already have very little access to fresh water.

Hot summer days can be great for having fun, but too much heat can be dangerous for some of us.

Heat Waves

We can expect more and more heat waves, when the temperature soars for days on end. To make ourselves comfortable, we'll be running our air conditioners on full blast, which can use as much energy as heating our homes in the winter. On the other hand, in many places we can expect more warm spells in the winter months, so we'll be using less energy to heat our homes. But the worst effect of extreme heat waves is not energy use — it's loss of life. In 2003 it got so hot in Europe that more than 20,000 people died from heat-related causes.

Mass Extinction

Many scientists believe that we're already in the middle of a mass extinction event, mostly caused by habitat destruction. With the added stress of changes caused by global warming, up to a quarter of all plant and vertebrate animal species could be at risk by the year 2050. We might be able to keep these numbers down by protecting habitats, particularly the ones scientists call "biodiversity hot spots." These are specialised habitats that contain a large number of species that couldn't move elsewhere, such as the tropical regions of the Andes mountains.

One third of all species of amphibian, including many poison dart frogs, are already under threat of extinction.

Lemurs, like the crowned one shown here, are not finding enough food because of changes in rainfall.

The Land

The Human Side...

Since most scientists agree that human-produced greenhouse gases are responsible for global warming, it's up to us to do something about it.

Alternative Energy Choices

The world's use of fossil fuels, and the amount of greenhouse gases they produce, continues to rise. One of the things we can do to slow this down is to shift over to alternative energy sources such as nuclear, solar or wind power, or even capturing methane from landfills and using it to generate electricity. And there are just as many alternative fuel choices being developed for vehicles (see below). Unfortunately, each of these choices has its own drawbacks, for instance, corn being grown for ethanol instead of for food. What we really need to do is to cut down on our use of all energy.

By the year 2020, half of all households in Europe will be powered solely by wind generators!

WHAT

Hydrogen

Vegetable Oil

Electricity

Algae Oil

Corn

Tree Planting

Trees, like all plants, take in CO_2 from the air. They use the carbon for their life processes, but release the oxygen. So plant trees! You don't have to do it yourself. You can donate to organisations that are planting trees all over the world, from Africa to the Amazon.

Over its lifetime, a single tree can absorb about 1 TONNE of CO_2.

There are more than 100,000 varieties of rice in the world!

Seeds of Life

With changing patterns of rainfall and worsening droughts, it will become more and more difficult to feed the world's growing population. To meet this challenge, agricultural experts are growing drought- and heat-resistant food crops by cross-breeding existing varieties and using bioengineering.

To protect plant diversity, many countries have been collecting seeds in "seed banks." Now, a huge one is being built into a mountain cave on an island high up in the Arctic. It will hold — and keep safe from disaster — every single known kind of food plant seed from around the world!

Over three million seeds will be kept frozen in Norway in what's been nicknamed "The Doomsday Vault".

People

As a species, we humans are responsible for producing far more than our share of greenhouse gases...

but we're also pretty clever,

People
Our Place on Earth

HUMAN POPULATION:

6,800,000,000

Yes, that's the right number: *6.8 BILLION*. And every single one of us wants to live in comfort. And we all need food. And we all need fresh water. And we all need homes, warmth and all kinds of other things.

FACT: Big animals are high energy consumers

...and *guess what?*

Humans are **BIG** animals

Our Energy Use

Heat

We've made ourselves at home everywhere on the planet, often in places that can be very cold. To keep ourselves warm in these cold places, we burn huge amounts of fuel — from wood to blocks of peat to natural gas.

Water

To use this natural resource, we have to pump it, clean it, heat it and then dispose of it when we're done with it — all things that require a lot of energy.

Food

The food we eat is a huge source of greenhouse gases. Fossil fuels are used in fertilisers and farm machinery, as well as for processing food, transporting it, packaging it and cooking it.

Construction

The construction industry uses all kinds of building materials, from wood to steel to concrete. Making concrete is a serious energy user, since its base must be heated to a very high temperature. All in all, our built environment accounts for almost half of the greenhouse gases we're responsible for.

Transportation

Until someone discovers the secret of teleportation, we're stuck with energy-consuming modes of transportation. Ships and planes are the worst greenhouse gas producers. Planes also create water vapour contrails behind them. This vapour contributes to warming by keeping heat from escaping into space.

Electricity

No, it's not magically captured by power cables. It's energy converted into electrical current. And that energy often comes from burning fossil fuels.

Manufacturing

All of the "things" in your life — from your clothes to your mobile phone to your toothbrush — have to be made. And making things uses energy. So does packaging those things.

People
We're All in This Together

One of the reasons humans have been so successful as a species is our use of natural resources, particularly our use of **fossil fuels**.

World CO₂ Emissions

Burning fossil fuels has been very **beneficial** for people. Imagine what it would be like to live without electricity or computers or cars. But the bad side is that we've added a lot of CO_2 to our atmosphere. And some of us have been adding a lot more than others. In fact, just ten countries, including China and the USA, contribute over 67% of the world's total CO_2 emissions.

Annual CO₂ emissions by country 2008 (in thousands of tonnes)

Rich Man, Poor Man

Some people in the world, particularly North Americans, use much more than their share of the world's resources, and so have a very big "**ecological footprint**". The world's poor have a much smaller footprint. But, of course, the poor want to live like the rich. This leaves us with a problem: For the world's poor to live like North Americans, not only would we need five planets' worth of natural resources, CO_2 emissions would soar. Maybe it's time the developed world managed with less.

The High Cost of Warming

Many people believe that to do nothing to slow the effects of global warming could end up costing much more than it will cost to control CO_2 emissions. Uncontrolled warming is guaranteed to increase the costs of flooding, water shortages, crop failures and insurance, though no one really knows how much these increases will be.

Kyoto Protocol

The Kyoto Protocol is an **energy pact** agreed on by more than a hundred countries. Developed countries that signed the pact have promised to drastically reduce their greenhouse gas emissions by the year 2012. So far, only a few of these countries expect to meet their goals. Some, such as the US, did not sign the pact, fearing that reducing emissions would not be good for their economy. But promising to follow agreements like the Kyoto Protocol will be absolutely necessary to slow global warming.

Global Action Plan

The international community needs to **join together** to combat warming. Together, we have to work out a way to burn far less fossil fuel, particularly in the developed world. The fossil fuels we *do* burn must be burned more efficiently and more cleanly, and the use of alternative energy sources has to be encouraged everywhere. And — because they process such huge quantities of CO_2 — it's also more important than ever to protect the world's forests and oceans.

Because trees absorb so much CO_2, it makes sense to protect the world's forests.

People
Human Ingenuity

Humans are the only sources of greenhouse gases on the planet that can actually **control** those sources. So, why don't we?

Scientists and inventors are coming up with lots of **fantastic plans** to help us control our greenhouse gas emissions. One scientist has discovered a type of algae that gobbles up both carbon dioxide and nitrous oxide (see page 19) from power plant exhaust. But that's not all — oil can then be squeezed out of the algae that can be used as a bio-fuel to run cars! Other scientists are capturing the Sun's energy using solar films that can be applied to building materials. And, in Italy, they've come up with a way to make compostable "bio-plastic" out of vegetable oil and starch!

Scientists have found a way to capture the Sun's energy in liquid form. Painted on glass, it could provide solar energy for houses. It might even be applied to fabrics, so you could charge personal electronics with the clothes you wear!

Zero-Energy Buildings

"Zero-energy" buildings use renewable energy, such as solar or wind power, are built from renewable resources, such as wood or even straw, and are super-insulated. Some people are going a step further and are designing "**living houses**". The walls and roof are formed from tree branches which are woven together. Rainwater and solar energy are used by both the living trees and the people inside the building. But best of all, fruiting plants can be grown on the outside, making the house edible!

Some architects are going beyond sod roofs like this one and are designing "living" houses constructed from growing trees.

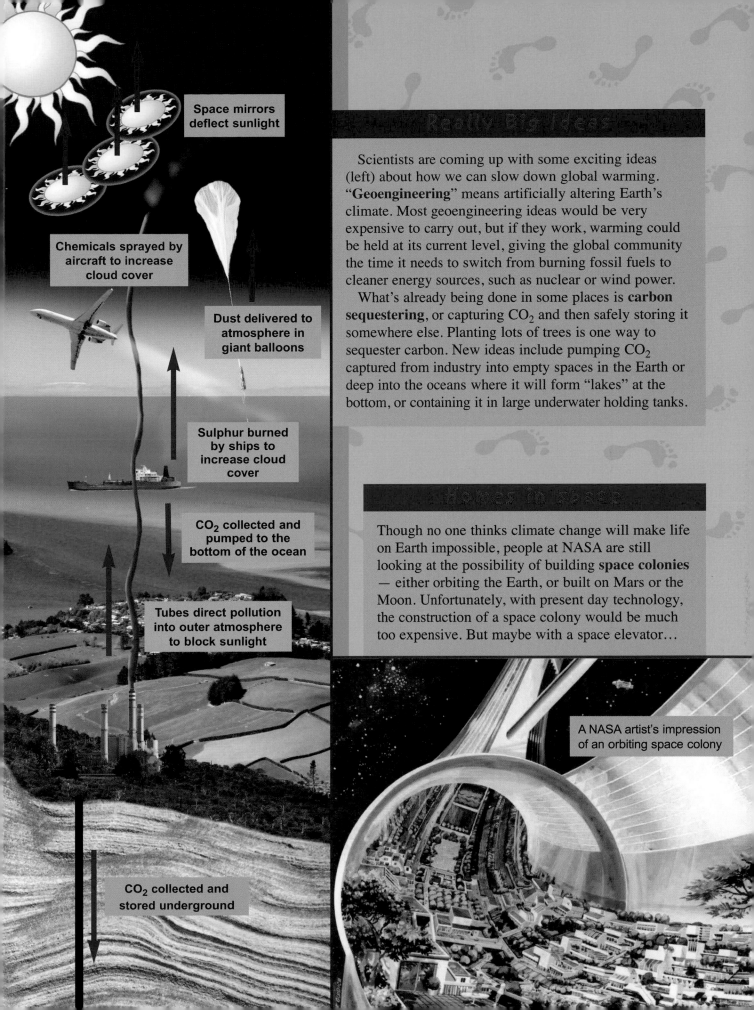

Space mirrors deflect sunlight

Chemicals sprayed by aircraft to increase cloud cover

Dust delivered to atmosphere in giant balloons

Sulphur burned by ships to increase cloud cover

CO_2 collected and pumped to the bottom of the ocean

Tubes direct pollution into outer atmosphere to block sunlight

CO_2 collected and stored underground

Really Big Ideas

Scientists are coming up with some exciting ideas (left) about how we can slow down global warming. "**Geoengineering**" means artificially altering Earth's climate. Most geoengineering ideas would be very expensive to carry out, but if they work, warming could be held at its current level, giving the global community the time it needs to switch from burning fossil fuels to cleaner energy sources, such as nuclear or wind power.

What's already being done in some places is **carbon sequestering**, or capturing CO_2 and then safely storing it somewhere else. Planting lots of trees is one way to sequester carbon. New ideas include pumping CO_2 captured from industry into empty spaces in the Earth or deep into the oceans where it will form "lakes" at the bottom, or containing it in large underwater holding tanks.

Homes in Space

Though no one thinks climate change will make life on Earth impossible, people at NASA are still looking at the possibility of building **space colonies** — either orbiting the Earth, or built on Mars or the Moon. Unfortunately, with present day technology, the construction of a space colony would be much too expensive. But maybe with a space elevator…

A NASA artist's impression of an orbiting space colony

People
What You Can Do

There's nothing stopping every single one of us from doing **small things** that can add up until they're big things.

As Easy as Changing a Light Bulb

One of the little things we can all do is to switch to **low-energy light bulbs**. This might not sound like it would make much of a difference, but if everyone on the planet made the switch to efficient lighting today, we would stop **16 billion tonnes** of carbon from entering the atmosphere over the next 25 years. That's a lot! Not only that, but when you make the switch, you also save money on your electricity bills!

The Three Rs

We're all doing lots of recycling, but we're still creating about **half a tonne of waste per person** each year in the UK. But there are still lots of ways to improve! You can donate usable items like clothes, toys and electronics to charitable organisations for redistribution. When you shop, look for minimal packaging. In Germany, the government charges both manufacturers and retailers a fee based on the amount of packaging they use. The result has been a big decline in rubbish. Shouldn't we do that everywhere?

When you ride a bike instead of travelling by car, you're doing something healthy for yourself – and for the planet!

Waste in landfills produces both CO_2 and methane.

Anti-Global-Warming Invention

The Jumper

It's Easy to Help!

When it's cold, turn the heating down and wear more clothes.

When it's hot, wear light clothes and use a fan instead of an air conditioner.

Turn out lights you're not using.

Turn your computer off and unplug chargers when not in use.

Only wash full loads of laundry.

Have a shower instead of a bath.

Walk, ride your bike or take public transport instead of asking for a lift in the car.

Plant a tree.

Don't buy bottled water. Drink tap water. Filter it if you like.

Eat lower on the food chain (more veg, less meat), and eat fewer processed foods.

Knowledge is Power

When you read about our global use of plastic water bottles (right), is it possible that you might think twice about buying water in plastic bottles? Change can't happen without knowledge, and knowledge comes from **reading** and **listening** and **discussing**. So learn all you can. Talk to your friends. Talk to your parents. Write a letter or email to your government representatives to ask what's being done. The more all of us learn about our environment, and how we affect it, the more willing each of us will be to make changes in our own lives.

Every year, 1.5 million tonnes of plastic is used to make plastic bottles. The manufacture and disposal of all that plastic adds to global warming and the plastic bottles themselves pollute our oceans.

This Is Everyone's Planet

If scientists are right, each one of us is at least a little bit responsible for global warming. And each one of us has to decide what kind of a world we want to live in in the future.

Our planet has been around for almost five billion years. In that time it has undergone **enormous change** over and over again. Global warming may be the Earth's next big change.

Humans are resilient, and Earth is, too!

No matter what changes lie ahead, the Earth isn't going anywhere. And neither are people. But what we do now could have a big effect on what our lives will be like in the years to come. **This is our planet!** Let's make sure it's as wonderful a place in the future as it is now.

Further information

The **Internet** is jam-packed with information about every topic touched on in this book. Find the most current information on a subject by typing in your key words such as "global warming adelie penguin" and then the year. Most of the following sites are designed for kids. The others are easy-to-understand and full of fascinating information.

Global warming:
http://www.bbc.co.uk/climate/
http://www.davidsuzuki.org/Climate_Change/
Earth:
http://kids.earth.nasa.gov/
Weather & Climate
http://www.bbc.co.uk/weather/weatherwise/factfiles/
Ecosystems:
http://www.mbgnet.net/index.html
Arctic:
http://www.arctic.noaa.gov/general.html

Oceans:
http://oceanexplorer.noaa.gov/
http://www.oceanlink.island.net/
Rainforests:
http://passporttoknowledge.com/rainforest/main.html
Endangered Species:
http://www.kidsplanet.org/
Renewable Energy
http://www.re-energy.ca/
Activism for Kids
http://www.youthactioncentre.ca/English/index.htm

Global Warming Books:
Planet Patrol Mick Manning and Brita Granström, Franklin Watts 2009
What's the Point of Being Green? Jacqui Bailey, Franklin Watts 2010

Acknowledgments

Without the generosity of a number of people, this book would not have been possible. These generous and thoughtful people include: Kendrick Taylor, Desert Research Institute, University and Community College System of Nevada, Claire Eamer, my brother, Bruce, my dad, Philip, and, my husband, Fred. I would also like to gratefully acknowledge the financial support of the Ontario Arts Council.

Index

acid 39
agriculture 19, 44, 51
    corn 50
    crop failure 15, 48, 57
    fertiliser 55
    food plants 51
    seed bank 51
albedo 24, 29
algae 36, 41, 50, 58
alternative energy
    biodiesel
    ethanol 50
    solar 50, 58, 59
    water 40
    wind 40, 50, 58, 59
amphibians
    frog 43, 49
    toad 33
Antarctic 20, 22-31
    new species 25, 45
Arctic 17, 22-31, 51
atmosphere 8, 9, 10, 11,
    16, 18-19, 20, 21, 29,
    35, 39, 44, 56, 59, 60
Australia 17, 44

bacteria 19
Bangladesh 38
biodiversity 9, 49
biofuel 29, 50
birds 6, 26, 29
    auklet 29
    duck 61
    penguin 18, 26
    robin 29
    sea 29, 35
    swallow 47
    warbler 27
    whitethroat 47
Bolivia 45
breeding 4, 26, 29, 46

Canada 44
carbon 29, 34, 50, 60
    cycle 10, 18-19
    dioxide (see green
    house gases)
    sequestering 59
    sink 10, 29, 34, 35, 44,
    45
carnivores 14
China 15, 56
climate 7, 12-13, 20-21,
    28
    Arctic 24
    models 21
construction 55
coral 20, 33, 36, 39, 41

decomposition10
deforestation 18, 45
Denmark 47
deserts 13, 44
dinosaur 13
disease 15

ecological footprint 56
ecosystem 14, 25, 26, 29,
    31, 35, 36, 37, 46
electricity 40, 50, 55, 60

low-energy lights 60
Europe 15, 28, 39, 46
extinction 28, 47, 49
erosion 30, 35, 41, 44

Finland 29
fire 16, 43, 44
fish 26, 31, 35, 36-37, 41
    fishing 31, 37, 40
    stocks 26, 37
    salmon 30
flooding 6,15, 17, 35, 38,
    41, 57
food 14, 35, 55
    shortage 15, 37, 49
food chain 14, 26, 35, 36,
    37
    plants 51
food web 14
forest 45, 57
    boreal 14, 27
    rainforest 45
fossils 35
fossil fuels 10, 18, 31, 50,
    55, 56, 57
    coal 10, 57
    natural gas 19, 55
    oil 10, 31

geoengineering 59
Germany 60
glacier 6, 11, 16, 17, 25,
    39, 45, 48
greenhouse effect 9, 18-19
greenhouse gases 9, 16,
    18-19, 20, 50 54, 56, 58
    carbon dioxide 9, 10,
    16, 18-19, 21, 34, 35,
    44, 50, 55, 56-57, 58,
    59
    methane 16, 19, 29,
    50, 60
    nitrous oxide 16, 19,
    58
    ozone 16
    water vapour 9, 11, 16,
    18
Germany 60
Greenland 20, 28, 45

habitat loss 47, 49
herbivores 14
Hockey Stick Graph 21

ice 11, 17, 18, 34
    berg 11, 17, 22, 25
    cap 11, 24, 28
    cores 20
    glacier 6, 11, 16, 17,
    25, 39, 45, 48
    sea 17, 24, 26, 27, 30,
    31
    sheet 25, 28
    shelf 25
Ice Age 13, 17, 21, 29
India 56
Indonesia 15, 44
industry 19
insects 6, 29, 46, 47
    beetles 27

butterfly 46
mosquito 15
termites 19
Inuit 22, 30
Italy 58

Kenya 48
krill 26, 35, 37
Kyoto Protocol 57

landfill 19, 50
Larsen B ice shelf 25
livestock 19
living things 10, 14
lobster 40

mammals 28, 37, 47
    bear 6, 47
    bear, polar 22, 27, 28
    caribou 30
    cat 15
    cow 10, 19
    fox 10
    gerbil 33
    lemur 49
    moose 27
    rabbit 10
    rat 15
    seal 27, 28, 30, 31, 37
    squirrel 27, 47
    tiger 47
    walrus 28
    whale 26, 31, 37
manufacturing 55, 61
mountains 13, 46

native peoples 30
North America 15, 39, 44,
    46, 56
Northwest Passage 31
Norway 51

ocean 11, 12, 16, 19, 32
    41, 57, 59
    carbon sink 10, 34, 35
    chemistry 34, 39
    circulation 34, 35
    currents 28, 29, 34, 39
    food chain 35, 36, 37
    sea water 35
oxygen 36, 51

packaging 55, 60
paleoclimatologists 20
peat 19, 29, 55
permafrost 25, 29, 30
photosynthesis 10,14, 34,
    36
plankton 26, 35, 37
    phytoplankton 34, 35,
    36
    zooplankton 35, 36, 39
plants 10, 11, 14, 29, 44,
    46, 49
    berries 29
    lichen 29
    photosynthesis 10, 34
    pollen 20
    seeds 51
plastic 58, 61

pollution 40
population 38, 50, 54, 56
Portugal 44
poverty 48, 56

refugees 38, 48
reptiles
    sea turtle 37
    gecko 15
rubbish 60

salt 31, 34
salt marsh 38, 41
sea level 17, 25, 28, 29,
    35, 37, 38
solar energy 8, 9, 14, 16,
    24, 58
solar radiation 8, 9
solar system 8
space colony 53, 59
Spain 47
species
    endangered
    invasive 37
    new 25
Sun 8, 58

temperature 7, 8, 9, 13,
    15, 16, 21, 24, 29
    ocean 29, 31, 36, 37,
    39
    surface 16
transportation 55
    bicycle 60
trees 25, 44, 45, 51, 58
    boreal forest 14, 27
    deforestation 18, 45
    mangroves 38, 41
    planting 51
    rainforest 45
    rings 20
    spruce 27
tundra 29

United States 56, 57

volcano 15, 18, 19

water 48
    cycle 11
    condensation 11
    evaporation 11, 17, 18
    shortages 57
    sublimation 11, 18
    transpiration 11
    vapour
weather 8,12, 13
    clouds 11
    drought 16, 17, 48, 51
    hail 12
    heat wave 16, 49
    hurricanes 9, 12, 17,
    33, 39, 41
    lightning 12
    precipitation 11, 12,
    15, 17, 45, 48, 51
    tornadoes 12
wetlands 29